OLYMPIC PENINSULA GOLD

Where to Find Gold on The Peninsula

A mining claim cabin still stands in 1983 in the Little River drainage of Olympic National Park. (Photo by M. Stupich.) Courtesy of National Park Service, Pacific Northwest Region

by

Dan Youra, Travel Writer

OLYGOLD.COM

Dedicated to Mom, my golden nugget

"Youra's coverage is hard to fault"
The Sunday Times of London

ABOUT THE AUTHOR

While writing articles for national and international clients, Dan Youra traveled the western hemisphere from Argentina to Alaska. After chasing gold stories from Machu Picchu in the Andes and Iquitos in the Amazon to the gold rush rivers of Alaska, he discovered the history of gold in his own backyard on the Olympic Peninsula in Washington State.

Travel writer by profession, Youra published the first *Mt. St. Helens Guide* after its eruption in 1980. He printed his first *Olympic Peninsula Map* in 1982 to celebrate the reopening of the Hood Canal Bridge. He wrote his premier *Olympic Peninsula Guide* in 1984. He was selected to publish the *Official Guidebook for the Washington State Pavilion* at EXPO 86 in Vancouver, B.C.

Youra's writing assignments have sent him to the jungles of Costa Rica by a European hotel chain and to the beaches of Cancun, Mexico by the Cancun Convention and Visitors Bureau and Mexico Secretary of Tourism. He worked in the press corps at the United Nations in New York, covered Congressional hearings in Washington, D.C. and published reports for the National Governor's Conference in San Juan, Puerto Rico.

Gold nuggets awarded to Youra include "PR whiz" from Emmett Watson, **Seattle Times**; "trailblazer" from Larry Coffman, **Marketing**; "pioneer in the Global Village" from Dan Evans, Governor of Washington; and, "life enhancing" from **The Sunday Times** of London.

Visit the author online at DanYoura.com.

PUBLISHER

Olympic Peninsula Gold: Where To Find Gold on the Peninsula is published by Youra Guides, P O Box 1169, Port Hadlock, WA 98339

Order online at **OlyCatalog.com.** To order wholesale copies send request to office@youra.com

ISBN 1442146613

EAN-13 9781442146617

© 2009 Youra Media. All rights reserved.

OLYMPIC PENINSULA GOLD

Where to Find Gold on The Peninsula

TABLE OF CONTENTS

INTRODUCTION	5
GOLD RUSH OF 1894	10
SEATTLE'S GOLD RUSH	11
MINING ON THE PENINSULA	15
OLYMPIC NATIONAL PARK	16
CLALLAM COUNTY	17
JEFFERSON COUNTY	21
MAP	24-25
GRAYS HARBOR COUNTY	26
MASON COUNTY	27
OLYMPIC BEACHES	29
GOLD BEARING BEACHES	31
INFORMATION AND RESOURCES	34
DEFINITION OF TERMS	39
ORGANIZATIONS	46
BIBLIOGRAPHY	47

by Dan Youra OlyGold.com

PREFACE

This book is published as part of the 2009 Olympic Peninsula Treasure Hunt and is designed in the format and theme of the 2009 Olympic Peninsula Treasure Hunt. The book is meant for the use and enjoyment of participants in the Olympic Peninsula Treasure Hunt.

The book brings together in one place the many reports from government agencies, articles and mining literature documenting the exploration, discover and extraction of gold and other minerals on Washington State's Olympic Peninsula. Some of the reports cited here were printed more than 150 years ago. The accuracy and reliability of some of the reports can be questioned and should not be interpreted as necessarily fully supported by facts. It is generally understood among gold prospectors that one does not eagerly share too much information about where and how much gold one finds.

The mining of gold placer deposits along the Olympic Peninsula's coast took place at a time preceding the establishment of Olympic National Park, the government agency which regulates the beaches along the northern Pacific coastline of the peninsula. Park rules govern access and activities on the beaches within the Park's jurisdiction and should be studied and adhered to by anyone considering looking for gold within the park's boundaries.

Washington State Laws also regulate mining activities and should be consulted prior to any mineral recovery efforts. See chapter on "Regulations" starting on page 35 in this book.

Dan Youra

May 1, 2009

INTRODUCTION

ALL THAT GLITTERS...

Myths and rumors about gold on Washington State's Olympic Peninsula have sparked the imaginations of curious treasure hunters for centuries. The search for gilded treasures hidden in its primeval forests and coastal coves began with the lore of British pirates and Spanish Conquistadors.

Many a campfire has flickered with tales of gold-laden galleons, knuckle-size nuggets, sunken safes and 24-carat beaches. The glint of the precious prize still spins its spell.

Does the abandoned Ruby gold mine near Kalaloch hide secrets to tell? Does gold still sluice in the beach sands at Shi Shi, Ozette and Yellow Banks? When the S.S. Governor sank off Port Townsend, how much gold was in her safe? Did Juan de Fuca really discover "gold, silver and pearls" as he claimed in the strait that bears his name?

PIRATE WARS

Gold stories started in the late 1500s, when King Phillip II of Spain and Queen Elizabeth of England at war with each other sent explorers, the other would say "pirates," to find and claim a Northwest Passage across the New World. The most renowned of the Queen's seamen, whom she granted a "privateering commission" was Francis Drake. With his license to plunder in hand, he set off in 1577 "to do maximum damage to the Spanish king's lands."

In 1578 Drake crossed the Strait of Magellan and entered the Pacific to harass the Spanish from the deck of Her Majesty's Golden Hind with her 22 guns and displacement of 300 tons. El Draque (The Dragon), as Drake was to be known to his Spanish victims, captured near Lima a Spanish ship laden with Peruvian gold valued at $10,000,000 by modern standards and captured off Ecuador Nuestra Senora de la Concepcion, a Spanish galleon with the colorful nickname Cacafuego. Her 26 tons of silver and 80 pounds of gold, valued at $12,000,000 at modern rates, took six days to transship and would be Drake's greatest prize.

With his plunder aboard Drake sailed north to the coastlines of present day Washington and British Columbia. The facts of Drake's voyage are sketchy at best, because Queen Elizabeth demanded secrecy of his bountiful quests. What happened to the ship logs? Many were lost and in 1698 a fire in Whitehall Palace burned the rest. Did Drake bury gold and silver along northwest beaches to lighten his load while charting straits and coves in search of the elusive passage?

In 1592 a Greek captain who called himself Juan de Fuca sailed under the flag of the Spanish Viceroy in Mexico and claimed to find "gold, silver and pearls" in his voyage on a northwest strait. Confronted with a threatening storm, Captain de Fuca's caravel, speculators think, had need to offload precious weight before it might sink. The strait that bears his name might still conceal de Fuca's buried gain.

Referred to in legend as a "most plausible liar," Juan de Fuca had other "peers as prevaricators" who sailed the peninsula's coast for the Spanish crown. Captain Lorenzo de Maldonado for one, and the "deep-sea liar" of even higher rank, Admiral Bartolome de Fone, who claimed to discover a great city on the strait, which he called the River of the Kings. The exploits of two pirates invite speculation about digging up treasures. The real hunt though becomes digging up the truth. But isn't that the nature of a treasure hunt?

"GLITTERING MOUNTAIN"

Two hundred years later the Spanish sent Captain Juan Perez to the northwest in 1774, where he sighted a "glittering mountain" rising from the dark mainland of what is now the Olympic Peninsula and named it Sierra de Santa Rosalia, a name that gave way to Mt. Olympus.

In the next two years Bruno Heceta made landfall at Destruction Island in view of the peninsula coast and claimed it for the King of Spain. A party of men was sent ashore to fetch fresh water but was ambushed and killed or captured by Indians. Were they rowing ashore to bury gold? The battered crew returned to Mexico.

In 1787 the Strait of Santa Rosalia was renamed the Strait of Juan de Fuca, named by the English Captain Charles William Barkley for the colorful Greek Captain who sailed its waters two centuries prior.

GIFTS OF THE GODS

Captain John Meares, aboard Felice, is credited with igniting the "Olympic" torch in the Northwest. In 1788, inspired by the grandeur of the peninsula's majestic mountains, Meares wrote his following famous words in the ship's log.

"If that not be the home where dwell the gods, it is certainly beautiful enough to be, and I therefore will call it Mt. Olympus."

The anointing of the Olympic Peninsula as "The Home of The Gods," ascribed a divine presence to the region and created a new treasure born from Greece's Golden Age, with its Olympic parthenon spawning Olympic games.

Captain Vancouver sealed the Olympic name for the peninsula three years after Meares, when he jotted "Olympic Peninsula" on the geographic region on one of his charts.

The richness of the Olympic treasure has grown to include a range of twenty-five mountain peaks on Mount Olympus, named for Greek, Roman and Norse gods. Local native Americans believed that the glacier-covered peak was the home of Thunderbird, their highest ranked totem.

GOLDEN BEACHES

As early as 1859 settlers reported traces of gold in the rivers draining out of the Olympic Mountains both to the north and to the south. By 1877 fairly reliable reports were published on the likelihood that gold would be found on the North Fork of the Skokomish River in Mason County.

In 1894 a report spread that pay sand could be found almost anywhere along the Olympic Coast from Cape Flattery to Grays Harbor. Successful claims were made at a number of beaches along the Pacific Coast of the Olympic Peninsula.

In 1928 J.T. Pardee described the gold on the Olympic Pacific coast. "Platinum and gold are found in a layer of heavy sand and gravel, concentrated by the waves on the beach at the foot of the sea cliff."

In his 1955 report on gold in Washington, M.T. Huntting lists gold-bearing beaches and brief notes on eleven beaches on the western beaches along the Pacific coast of the Olympic Peninsula. The author of *Exploring and Mining Gems and Gold in the West* includes "the savage wilderness and rain forests of the Olympic Peninsula in Washington."

MINING REGULATIONS

In order to prospect for gold and other minerals in Washington State, a prospector must know the rules governing mineral extraction. For answers about the laws download "Gold and Fish: Rules and Regulations for Mineral Prospecting and Placer Mining" published by Washington Dept. of Fish and Wildlife.

LOGGING

Harriet U. Fish in *Tracks, Trails and Tales*, notes that one of the earliest lumber operations and sawmills took root in 1852. The California gold rush had a direct bearing upon the growth of the lumber industry and sawmills of the Pacific Northwest, during the 1850s and 1860s. In fact, most of the mills around Puget Sound and the Strait shores, were California built, owned and operated.

SUNKEN TREASURES

Stories of sunken treasures aboard sunken ships abound around the Olympic Peninsula and Puget Sound.

From the *S.S. Pacific* ship wrecked off Neah Bay to the *S.S. Governor* sunk off Port Townsend, hauling gold in her safe as part of her payload, glints of gold from their watery tombs spark flights of fancy to fill a treasure hunter's chest.

Where do tall tales end and facts begin? What would you expect to find on Gold Creek trail near Sequim? Is the gold dust on peninsula beaches from nearby gold mines or from pirates who buried Spanish doubloons? Is the gold from a sunken ship's safe? Or, is it simply fools gold reflecting the lure of riches in the eye of the beholder?

GOLD RUSH - 1894

A brief excitement over beach placers on Washington's Olympic Peninsula might qualify as the region's last gold rush. In 1894, a report spread that pay sand could be found almost anywhere along the Olympic Coast from Cape Flattery to Gray's Harbor. Gold-seekers rushed to the coast and staked most of the sand beaches for a length of sixty to seventy miles. Successful operations were limited to three claims -at Shi Shi Beach, Yellow Banks, and a point about two miles south of the mouth of the Ozette River. Miners worked these claims by sluicing primarily, water being taken from nearby streams and conveyed by wooden flume to the sluice boxes, or by rocker where the water supply was limited. By 1905, an estimated $15,000 in gold had been extracted from the beach sands."

These rushes were like earlier rushes in that miners needed little more than a grubstake and some simple tools to work the gold out of the earth. By contrast, deep placer and lode mining required more sophisticated technology and much larger investments of capital.

SEATTLE'S GOLD RUSH

In August 1896 when Skookum Jim Mason, Dawson Charlie and George Washington Carmack found gold in a tributary of the Klondike River in Canada's Yukon Territory, they had no idea they would set off one of the greatest gold rushes in history. Beginning in 1897, an army of hopeful gold seekers, unaware that most of the good Klondike claims were already staked, boarded ships and Seattle and other Pacific port cities and headed north toward the vision of riches to be had for the taking.

The Klondike stampede was perhaps the single most dramatic event in Pacific Northwest history. It made Seattle a household word around the world, luring an estimated 30,000 Klondike-bound fortune-seekers and transforming a frontier port into a booming metropolis.

The commercial history of Seattle is built upon the backs of the miners who went north to strike it rich in Alaska's Klondike Gold Rush of 1897. The business barons of Seattle found their own gold in "mining the miners." By selling supplies to outfit the miners, some of Seattle's greatest names in retail got their start in the gold rush that built the financial foundation for Puget Sound's Emerald City.

John W. Nordstrom heeded the call of the wild and an itch for gold. After two years in the Klondike he earned $13,000 in a gold mine and returned to the northwest to start his first store in downtown Seattle.

Gold seekers in Seattle board the Portland, bound for the Klondike. (Courtesy National Park Service)

In July 1897, the steamship Portland arrived with a cargo of gold. In the weeks that followed, and throughout the Klondike Gold Rush, Seattle dominated the outfitting trade. Thousands of people from across the United States the world arrived to purchase tons of food, clothing and equipment and to book passage north. Guidebooks and newspapers lauded Seattle's facilities. The Chicago Record boasted that "the outfits purchased in Seattle by twenty experienced miners on the way to the Klondike are regarded as models by miners who have returned from that region."

Many stampeders arrived in Seattle by train and left for the gold fields on a ship. Seattle's role in the gold rush was defined, in part, by its role as a transportation center. Until the coming of the Great Northern and Northern Pacific Railroads, Seattle's most reliable connection to the outside world was by sea. City leaders lobbied for a transcontinental rail link to ship timber and imported goods east in exchange for finished goods and passenger service. By 1897, the region had steamship service north to Alaska and rail service over the Cascade Mountains as well as north to Vancouver, British Columbia and south to San Francisco and Los Angeles, California.

Seattle's success as an outfitting and transportation center was due in part to geography and economic conditions. The rest was due to an aggressive marketing campaign. Seattle's merchant community recognized the opportunity that the Klondike Gold Rush represented and embarked upon a media blitz with an extraordinary reach. In the weeks following the arrival of the *S.S. Portland* in Seattle, the Chamber of Commerce and merchants formed a Klondike Advertising Committee. The wealth and fame that Seattle gained during the gold rush is, in large part, the result of this committee and the efforts of its intrepid leader, Erastus Brainerd.

The image of stampeders and merchants in Seattle as white males of European descent is only partially true. Seattle by 1897 was home to Asian, African-American, and diverse European cultures, many of whom worked as outfitters or left to go to the Gold Fields. Women who made the trek north found jobs in a variety of places, including saloons and dance halls; many also started their own businesses including bakeries, laundries, restaurants, and hotels. In Skagway and along the northern trails, many coastal Indians worked as guides, packers, and traders. The choices below tell the stories of several people involved in the Rush.

As a result of the Gold Rush, Seattle earned a reputation as the commercial center of the Pacific Northwest. In the decade following the rush, the population doubled and the city expanded to the surrounding hills. Gold Rush tax revenues financed comprehensive water and sewage systems, the locks between Lake Washington and Lake Union, and regrades of the steep hills and wetlands in the downtown area. In 1909, Seattle celebrated its new fame with the Alaska-Yukon-Pacific Exposition.

The Klondike stampede boosted Seattle's shipping to the Far North considerably. According to a newspaper report, Seattle's fleet tripled in size between 1897 and 1898, in part due to the "Alaskan business." So pressing was the demand for steamships in the late

1890s that some vessels of marginal quality were placed in service. Seattle's shipping "never was so entirely engaged," explained one reporter in 1897. "Not a single vessel seaworthy and capable of use" was overlooked.

During the late nineteenth century, shippers filled these vessels to capacity. The Alaska Steamship Company, for instance, operated vessels that carried as many as 700 passengers apiece. In general, each ship ran between Seattle and the Far North one and one-half times per month. To prospector Martha Louise Black, it seemed that steamships left Seattle for Alaska "almost every hour." The historian Clarence B. Bagley noted that all this activity resulted in a "scene of confusion" on the Seattle waterfront that "has never been equaled by any other American port." The docks were piled high with outfits, and crowds of impatient miners "anxiously sought for some floating carrier to take them to the land of gold."

Shipping continued to expand in Seattle during the subsequent gold rush to Nome in 1899-1900. By that time, according to Bagley, the city's fleet had become a "great armada." He detected an interesting trend: at the end of the nineteenth century, only 10 percent of the ships sailing from Seattle to Alaska were owned and operated by people based in Seattle. In 1905, however, more than 90 percent of the vessels sailing from Seattle to Alaska were controlled by Seattle residents and businesses based in the city.

On July 25, 1897, author Jack London, under the spell of the gold fever, boarded a ship in San Francisco along with other prospectors bound for Port Townsend on the Puget Sound. From there he made his way to Juneau, Alaska and through the mountains to the Klondike. The author's experiences on this adventure became the subject of his world-renowned novels.

MINING ON THE PENINSULA
HISTORY

The history of manganese mining in the Olympics is more complicated. The existence of iron, copper, and manganese deposits was known as early as 1880, but the familiar problems of transportation and supply inhibited development for many years. Interest in the manganese deposits was heightened during World War II; however, the areas in which the claims occurred were then within Olympic National Park (established 1938), creating a dubious administrative environment for mining exploration.

Manganese deposits were found in a horseshoe-shaped mineral belt around the east, north, and west sides of the Olympic Mountains. Mining focused on four areas: Elwha River Valley, Little River/Hurricane Ridge, Lake Crescent area, and North Fork of the Skokomish River Valley. The latter included the earliest mines (late 1880s or early 1890s) and the most persistent operations (into the 1940s). Details are in *Historic Resource Study: Olympic National Park WA* (1983), Gail E. H. Evans and T. Allan Comp.

The mining tailings from the Black and White Mine remain as a testament to the persevering efforts of hard rock miners who sought to extract "paying" quantities of manganese and copper from the mountainside above the North Fork Skokomish River. Recent fire destroyed timber in the area. (Photo by R. Keatts.)

OLYMPIC NATIONAL PARK
MINING ACTIVITY

Residents of the Olympic Peninsula long suspected that the Olympic Mountains contained rich deposits of gold and other precious minerals. As early as 1859 and 1861, settlers reported traces of gold in the rivers draining out of the mountains both to the north and south, and by 1877 fairly reliable reports were published on the likelihood that gold would be found on the North Fork of the Skokomish River. Even more than in the North Cascades, however, difficulties of terrain in the Olympic Mountains inhibited exploration and development. As a result, the park has a long history of prospecting and a comparatively short history of mine development and extraction. Much of the prospecting and mining in the Olympic Mountains occurred under the stimulus of the two world wars and focused on manganese.

The manganiferous deposits occur in a mineral belt along the outer slopes of the Olympic Mountains on the north, south, and east. Generally they are found in heavily timbered country below an altitude of 4,000 feet. At two locations - near Humptulips and around Lake Crescent - the deposits occur at somewhat lower elevations. These conditions made prospecting unusually difficult, for travel through the dense forests was arduous and the search for outcrops was encumbered by a thick carpet of moss covering nearly everything. Not surprisingly, one of the earliest discoveries in this mineral belt was made near Lake Crescent where rock outcroppings had been laid bare.

While prospectors swarmed all over the Olympic Peninsula at the end of the 19th century, actual mining claims were confined primarily to 5 areas in what is now Olympic National Park: two on the north, one on the southeast, one on the south, and one along the park's coastal strip where beach placers were found.

CLALLAM COUNTY
ELWHA / LITTLE RIVER / HURRICANE RIDGE

In 1897 or 1898, Ward Sanders and Will and Martin Humes found prospects on a ledge about 325 feet above the Elwha River, west of Hurricane Hill. Other prospectors located claims in the same area. When the newly proclaimed Olympic Forest Reserve was surveyed at the turn of the century, the U.S. Geological Survey report noted mining activity in the Hurricane Ridge area. In the early 1900s, M. J. Gregory opened a mine in the Little River drainage southwest of Mount Angeles. By 1917, Gregory's mine consisted of four tunnels ranging from 40 to 210 feet in length.

During the next few years, several lode claims were made west of Mount Angeles in what was known as the Little River or Hurricane Mining District. These claims centered on the manganese belt. A 1934 survey by a state mining engineer recorded some 26 claims in the district, clustered on Hutton Ridge at an elevation of 4,200 to 5,000 feet above sea level. Some claims were developed with mine entrances.

Access to the district was by pack trail. During World War II, the mineral claimants apparently asked the state to survey a mine-to-market road but the cost was prohibitive. The difficulty of transporting the ore was never surmounted and one by one the claims were abandoned.

Little physical remains are left. At least two miner's cabins were located in the district, one on "Whistler Flat" at an elevation of 3,200 feet, as recorded by the state mining engineer in 1934; the second located on the Elwha River approximately 4 miles from the Little River trailhead. The latter cabin, called the Skookum Mining Claim Cabin, was inventoried in 1983.

LAKE CRESCENT

Theodore F. Rixon, Caroline Rixon, and Charles Anderson located three manganese lode claims on the south slope of Mount Muller about 1.25 miles west of Lake Crescent in September 1923. A partnership called Jamison and Peacock of Duluth, Minnesota leased the claims and developed the mine between 1924 and 1926. Ore production began in 1924 and amounted to 11,000 tons by September 1925. Most of the ore went by railroad to Port Angeles and then by ship via the Panama Canal to Philadelphia where it was used in making steel.

Underground workings of the Crescent Mine consisted of four mines at descending elevations on the slope of Mount Muller, with raises and slopes between them. The ore body formed a nearly vertical tabular mass from 6 to 14 feet thick with a maximum pitch length of 180 feet and a maximum stope length of 120 feet. The main slope was situated above the No. 3 mine and was almost completely worked out by September 1925.

From the main mine, No. 3, at an elevation of about 1,800 feet, the ore was transferred to a bin at the foot of the slope, 750 feet below, via a single-span aerial tramway 1,400 feet in length. From the bin the ore was loaded directly onto railroad cars. The railroad, known as the Lyon & Hill Railway when the mine was producing in the 1920s, was formerly operated by the U.S. Army's Spruce Production Division. Other surface structures at the Crescent Mine included wood frame cabins, blacksmith shop, powder house, and compressor house.

Peacock and Jamison suspended operations in 1926 and the property passed to the Washington Manganese Corporation. In 1929, the U.S. Bureau of Mines conducted exploratory deep drilling at the site as part of its strategic mineral inventory.

World War II caused renewed interest in the manganese deposits in the Olympic Mountains, and the Crescent Mine entered another period of production. The Sunshine Mining Company leased the property in 1941 and produced more than 10,000 tons of ore by 1945. A report in 1942 stated that the lowest level in the mine had 2,900 feet of drifts and crosscuts, largely in basalt. The mine was still producing as late as 1960, but in 1983 "two readily visible tunnels, mining tailings, and three or four collapsed and deteriorating buildings [were] the only remaining evidence of the once robust manganese mining operation."

East of the Crescent Mine the ledge was traced to the end of the Mount Muller ridge at the bend in Lake Crescent. Geologist J. T. Pardee reported four lode claims, the Peggy, Charles G., Charles A., and Mother Lode, on outcroppings along the ledge at points east, in 1927. All were on the same south-facing slope, but at lower elevations. Outcroppings of the manganiferous deposit were located at points west of the Crescent Mine, too, but these sites lie outside the park boundary.

State geologist Stephen H. Green described a slightly different complex of claims in a 1945 report. According to Green, the Peggy claim was located about 1,300 feet northeast of the Crescent mine entrance, the Daisy claims were situated in the southwest corner of Section 19 (Township 30-9W) at an elevation of about 2,100 feet. The Daddy and Mother claims were located side by side above the county road to Ovington, with the common discovery post located "67 feet east and 7 feet north of the southwest corner of lot 4, sec. 30 (30-9W)."

Green listed two other sites in the Aurora Ridge area within the park boundary. He noted three manganese deposits on the North Slope of the ridge at approximately 4,200 feet elevation. One ore body was exposed for an estimated vertical distance of 175 feet on the face of a high bluff. And just below the crest of Aurora Ridge, about 1 1/2 miles west of Lizard Head Peak, lay the Bertha claim.

ENNIS CREEK

South of Port Angeles, between Ennis Creek and the head of White Creek, on Melick Farm, in section 23 T30N R6W, is the Port Angeles Mine. This was a lode gold mine. If you go Southeast 6 miles and 3.5 miles by trail, on Cowan Creek, a tributary to the Little River, in section 6 T29N R6W, is the location of the Angeles Star Mine.

ARCH-A-WAT

Arch-A-Wat is located W of Neah Bay, on the Pacific Ocean. Access to the property is on the Makah Indian Reservation and is subject to the regulations of the tribe. If you go south of Arch-A-Wat along the beach to between Portage Head and Point of Arches, in sections 18, 19 and 30, T32N R15W, you will find the Shi Shi Beach (Lovelace) Placer Mine. The road from Neah Bay reaches a place on the cliff above the beach where there are some productive placers. Gold, platinum, iridium and zircon can be found. Two miles north of the mouth of the Ozette River, section 12 T31N R16W, is the location of the Ozette Beach Placer. You can access it from a trail from the Little Ozette River. Gold and Platinum can be found here.

In T30N R15W at the mouth of Little Wink Creek, in the S 1/2 of the SW 1/4 section 1, is the location of the Little Wink Placers. Also near a small stream in the NW 1/4 of the NW 1/4 section 19, The Main and Barnes Placer, which consisted of fine gold, platinum, silver, zircon. At high tide level in SW 1/4 of the SW 1/4 of section 18, is the Morrow Placer, consisting of flour gold. 2 miles south of Sand Point, in SW 1/4 section 18 is the Yellow

Banks Placer, which consisted of gold, platinum. You can reach it by hiking along beach from Ozette River mouth or north from La Push.

LA PUSH

North of La Push 4 miles along beach, at Johnson Point (Cape Johnson) in the NW 1/4 Section 5 T28N R15W, is the Johnson Point Placer. In the beach black sands and adjacent bench black sand deposits you can find placer gold and platinum. North of La Push 10 miles along beach, near mouth of Cedar Creek, in the E 1/2 of section 18 T29N R15W, is the Cedar Creek Placers. You can find very fine gold here. In section 19, black sand beach deposits contain gold and platinum. North on the beach 125 feet NW of the mouth of Big Wink Creek in NW 1/4 of NW 1/4 of the NE 1/4 section 12 T30N R16W is the Morgan Placers.

JEFFERSON COUNTY
KALALOCH BEACH

Kalaloch Beach in eastern Jefferson County was a gold producer and is about the furthest southern point along the western shore of the Olympic Peninsula where active placer sediments were found. See historical photo on front cover of early miners on Kalaloch Beach.

An abondoned gold mine shows up in records around Ruby Beach north of Kalaoch Beach. See Forks information center for directions.

North of Kalaloch to Ruby Beach, on tombolo between Abbey Island and Ruby Beach, in E 1/2 of NE 1/4 section 31 T26N R13W, in black sand deposits you can fine some very fine grained gold.

HOW DID SILVER, GOLD AND COPPER CREEKS GET THEIR NAMES?

Many locals, according to Harriet U. Fish in her book *The Lure of the Tubal-Cain*, have surmised that some early prospector gave the creeks these names from hope, anticipation, or the actual finding of these desired metals within the rushing waters. But the true story as told by Eva Cook Taylor, or "Mule Rider" as she was typically called from wandering the Jefferson County mountains and valleys both on mules and on foot as a teenager, was that in the 1890s, young Silas Marple of Brinnon, during his explorations of the crags and ridges of the Iron Mountain area, had named most of these creeks.

The names came from the high quality assays of metals he had recovered in his wanderings. Because of this, he filed a claim on the mountain's steep slope in 1901. So sure was he of the potential, he interested "city" men to join him, as they had funds with which to develop the mining processes. So, in 1903 The Tubal-Cain Copper and Manganese Mining Company was formed.

THE TUBAL-CAIN MINE

In Eva Taylor's book *The Lure of the Tubal-Cain*, she refers to the early men who located, planned, dreamed, and designed the routes into the mine area, who lugged the materials, did the engineering, constructed the mine buildings, and "worked" the outcroppings of manganese and copper, which were obvious along these mountain ridges.

Tubal-Cain Mine

The name Tubal-Cain comes from Genesis 4:22 and means a skilled workman, a smith who forges sharp cutting tools of bronze and iron.

An article in the *Port Townsend Leader* of June 14, 1903, raved about "A Monster Ledge of Iron" having been discovered. Over the next years the physical outlay to mine this was gigantic and the manganese and copper outcroppings seemed of high quality and worth the effort. Tunneling and mining continued between 1911 and 1915, with the men working through winters to maintain their investments. conditions finally proved insurmountable: snow slides wrecked buildings, the ruggedness of terrain, weather and broken outcroppings contributed to the abandonment of the effort. The veins never did reveal the amount of ore anticipated.

According to Harriet Fish in September 1980, the ores are there, with high assays, and the ever eager dream of a great strike still lurks, but has only been found in small and scattered amounts. The names of the Copper, Silver and Gold Creeks help to maintain enthusiasm and anticipation.

To see full size, 4-color map on web visit www.OlyTreasure.com.

OlyGold.com   24   Olympic Peninsula Gold

oria, B.C.

of Discovery
-2009

Vancouver B.C.
HMS Discovery
Capt. George Vancouver
Entered Strait
April 29,

Dungeness Spit
Port Townsend
Protection Is.
Discovery Bay
S.S. Governor

Sequim

Jamestown S'Klallam Tribe

uan Perez sighted ering mountain"

Chimacum Tribe

S'Klallam Tribe

nsula

Suquamish Tribe

Hood Canal

Seattle

Lake Cushman

Tacoma

Skokomish Tribe

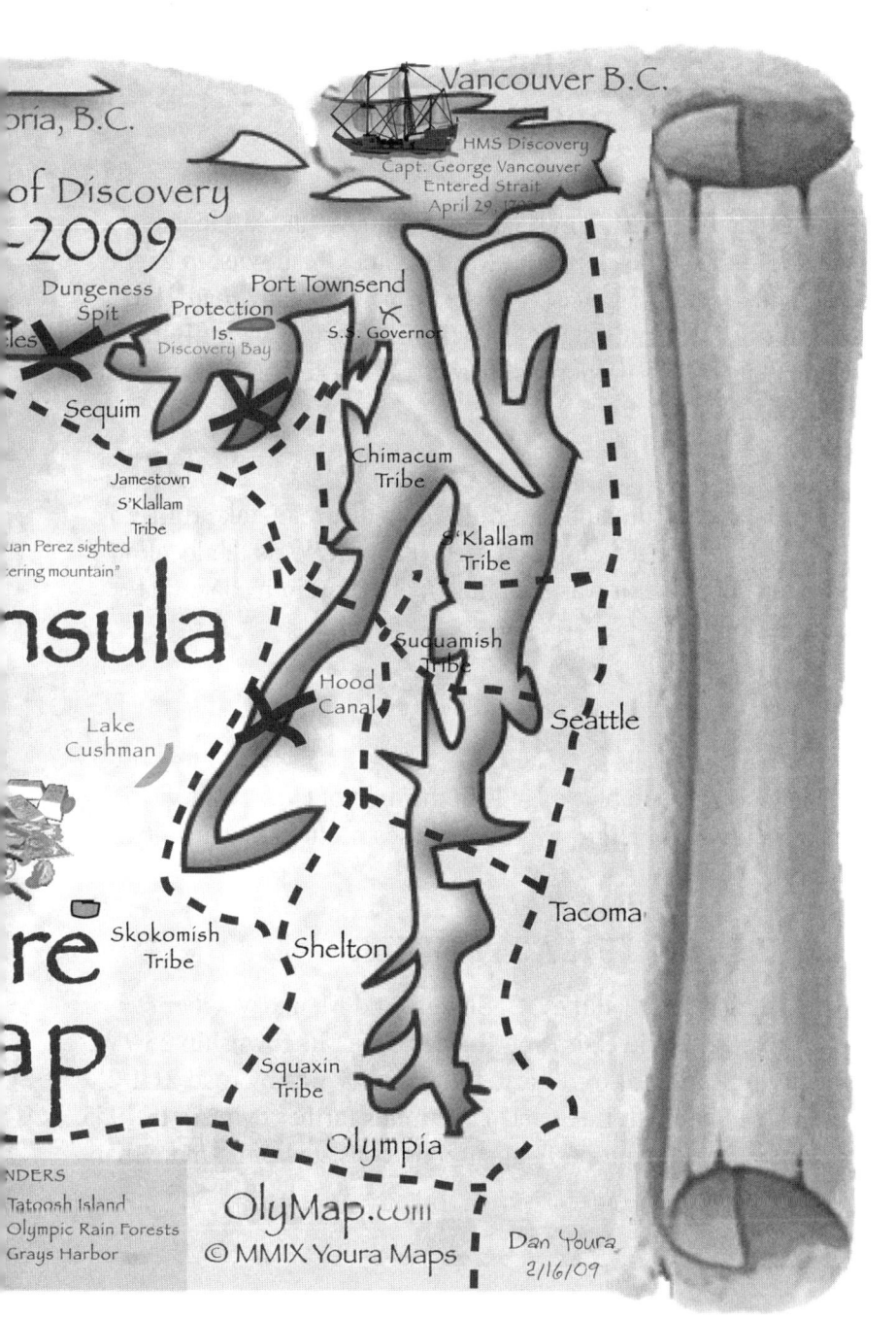

Shelton

Squaxin Tribe

Olympia

NDERS
Tatoosh Island
Olympic Rain Forests
Grays Harbor

OlyMap.com
© MMIX Youra Maps

Dan Youra
2/16/09

To order map online visit www.OlyCatalog.com

by Dan Youra   25   OlyGold.com

GRAYS HARBOR COUNTY
RUSTLER CREEK

M. H. and P. A. Mulkey, C. Slough, and M. and V. Oberg owned five gold lode claims on Rustler Creek in Township 25-7W, possibly in Section 31. Access to the property was by road 21 1/2 miles above Quinault Lake and 1 1/2 miles farther by trail. In 1955, development of this property apparently consisted of no more than an open cut.

Northeast of Quinault 22.5 miles on a dirt road, take trail 1.5 miles, on Rustler Creek, in section 31 T25N R7W, is the location of the Rustler Mine. It was 5 claims in quartz vein in slate that produced lode gold.

MOCLIPS

The ocean beach black sands in the area of Cow Point yield gold. Moclips is on Highway 109 20 miles north of Ocean City.

NORTH FORK QUINAULT RIVER

M. H. and P. A. Mulkey, C. Slough, and M. and V. Oberg owned five gold lode claims on Rustler Creek in Township 25-7W, possibly in Section 31. Access to the property was by road 21 1/2 miles above Quinault Lake and 1 1/2 miles farther by trail. In 1955, development of this property apparently consisted of no more than an open cut.

OYHUT

Oyhut ocean beach black sands contain gold.

MASON COUNTY
NORTH FORK SKOKOMISH RIVER

Some 400 mineral claims were located in the North Fork of the Skokomish River between 1890 and about 1940, but little remains of these workings today.

Prospectors discovered rich iron deposits on the North Fork of the Skokomish River as early as 1871, and manganese deposits had been reported by 1880. With the discovery of copper ore in the late 1880s, interest in the area grew. In 1890, the Mason County Mining and Development Company led by F. H. Whitworth of Seattle began to develop a copper and iron mine in the area. A writer for the Mason County Journal reported in August 1890 that a "gang of men...[were] hard at work blasting and working out the rich red ore." By then another company headed by John S. Soule of Grays Harbor had located seven other claims and was pushing development. When members of the Joseph G. Weil expedition passed through the area that year they found a substantial trail and mining camp.

Meanwhile, prospectors had staked other claims higher on the North Fork near the mouth of Seven Stream. Smith Keller, Joseph Moss, and George Thomas were three of the most persistent developers, apparently returning to the mine each summer for a period of weeks over a span of several decades. In 1935 or 1936, Joseph Moss formed the North Fork Mining Company with five partners and filed 17 claims near the mouth of Nine Stream Creek. In the 1940s, the original was known as the Smith Keller or Lucky Wednesday mine.

A short distance up the river from the Lucky Wednesday Mine, on the east side, a man named Chris Hammer had a cabin and several claims. Hammer came to the valley from Alaska in 1909. He sold two claims to Erie S. Snyder in 1912, and continued to work his other claims for eight more years. When he died in his cabin in 1920 he had six claims. These were acquired by the State of Washington in 1923 in probate court for unpaid taxes.

The Brown Mule Mine was operated by the Triple Trip Mining Company sometime prior to 1915. It was located on Copper Creek about 1/4 mile from the North Fork. Some entrances are all that remained of the mine in 1980.

Another long-lived but ultimately unsuccessful mine was the Black and White. In 1907, Wilhelm F. Nelson located two claims called the Kuger and Three Friends at about 4,000 feet elevation on the East Side of the North Fork drainage. Later that year Nels C. Christiansen filed two nearby claims, the Three-in-One and Peerless, while George B. Conway and Frank B. Standard located a fifth claim, the Arkansas Traveler. These five claims comprised what became known as the Black and White Mine. The developers of the mine pinned their hopes on the copper values in the ore, but the mine's inaccessibility high above the river valley prevented them from ever attracting a large investment.

In 1912, the Olympian Copper Company requested permission from the Forest Service to use downed timber for the construction of a flume in which the ore would be transported. Although this flume was apparently never built, 5 tons of ore were somehow shipped from the mine to the Tacoma smelter in 1915, and 100 more tons were shipped to the Bilrowe Alloys Company of Tacoma about three years later. In 1919, the developers tried unsuccessfully to sell the property for $150,000.

State Mining Engineer Stephen Green visited the property in 1945 and reported that development work at the Black and White

Mine consisted of a 200-foot tunnel, a 40-foot shaft, and several pits and open cuts. During the 1950s and 1960s, a miner's cabin at the site saw occasional use by recreational hikers. By the 1970s this cabin had collapsed and by the 1980s only the foundation logs remained.

Another mine operation was begun on the Black Queen group of claims, located about 1/4 mile above the mouth of Copper Creek on the West Side of the North Fork. State Mining Engineer Stephen Green reported in 1945 that the site included a shallow shaft and several open cuts. Directly across the river, another group of claims known as the Hi Hopes group were filed in 1940 and an adit was driven 50 feet into the hillside. The latter workings were in disrepair by 1942.

Finally, Green noted the Smith Mine a mile southeast of the Black and White. The claims were originally staked in 1914, and Green had no information on the size or content of the lode.

OLYMPIC BEACHES
CAPE FLATTERY AND SOUTH

During a brief gold excitement in 1894, the Olympic beaches were staked for 60 to 70 miles south of Cape Flattery. The productive localities were soon found to be within a 20-mile stretch from Portage Head, about 8 miles south of Cape Flattery, to Cape Johnson, a short distance north of the Quillayute River. The most productive site was Shi Shi Beach, at the north end of this strip. Smaller placers were worked at Ozette Beach and Yellow Banks - the latter by a miner named D. J. Wright who was using a rocker as late as 1917.

Perhaps the last locality to be developed was at the mouth of Sunset Creek, 6 miles north of the Quillayute. There a miner named J. M. Starbuck reported in 1917 that he had produced about $5,000 gold and five ounces of crude platinum up to that time.

SHI SHI BEACH

J. T. Pardee's description of the placer deposit at Shi Shi Beach in 1928 is suggestive of the labor involved in extracting the gold:

> Platinum and gold are found in a layer of heavy sand and gravel, concentrated by the waves on the beach at the foot of the sea cliff.
>
> At Shi Shi Beach, the wave terrace, which forms the bedrock of the deposit, is cut in sandstone of the older series of rocks, the upper part of the cliff being composed of Pleistocene gravel and drift.
>
> The beach is covered with a layer of fine gravel and sand from 1 to 3 feet thick and is strewn with cobbles at the base of the cliff.
>
> The metal-bearing part of this deposit is a thin layer of fine, heavy sand, composed chiefly of pink garnet and black grains of ilmenite and magnetite, and lies next to the bedrock.
>
> During storms the gravel and sand are shifted back and forth more or less, and some of the workable deposits may be buried or swept away and others may be uncovered as a result of the shifting.
>
> Part of the gold and platinum has worked down into joints and seams of the bedrock, the top layer of which, therefore, forms part of the pay streak.

Men seek their fortune at this early 1920s gold mining operation on the Pacific Ocean beach north of Kalaloch Creek. (Photo by A. Curtis.)

GOLD BEARING BEACHES
MARSHALL T. HUNTTING 1955 REPORT

In his 1955 report on gold in Washington, Marshall T. Huntting provided a list of gold-bearing Olympic beaches and brief notes on each. From north to south, these were as follows:

SHI SHI BEACH a.k.a. Lovelace Placer Located between Portage Head and Point of Arches in Sections 18, 19, and 30 (32-15W). Accessed by road from Neah Bay to top of sea cliff.

OZETTE BEACH, Ozette Beach Placers. Located two miles north of the mouth of the Ozette River in Section 12 (31-16W). Accessed by trail from Lake Ozette.

LITTLE WINK PLACER a.k.a. Japanese, Sand Point placers. Located at the mouth of Little Wink Creek in Section 1 (30-16W)) and accessed by trail.

MORGAN PLACER, a.k.a. Big Wink Creek Placer. Located 125 feet northwest of the mouth of Big Wink Creek in Section 12 (30-16W), and accessed by trail. Development consisted of a pit 30 feet long by 15 feet wide by 6 feet deep.

MORROW PLACER. Located in SWI/4 SW 1/4 of Section 18 (30-15W) at high-tide level. An area 50 feet by 25 feet was worked from 1932 to 1940 and reportedly produced as much as $1,678 in one year.

YELLOW BANKS PLACER. Located two miles south of Sand Point in SW 1/4 Section 18 (30-15W). Accessed by biking along beach south from Ozette Beach or north from La Push.

MAIN AND BARTNERS PLACER. Located in NW 1/4 NW 1/4 of Section 19 (30-15W) near a small stream. Accessed by trail. Development consisted of an irregular pit 30 feet long by 15 feet wide and 6 feet deep, and a flume 150 feet long.

JOHNSON POINT PLACER. Located in NW 1/4 of Section 15 (28-15W) at Johnson Point, or Cape Johnson. Accessed by hiking along beach from La Push.

STARBUCK PLACER, a.k.a. Cedar Creek Placer. Located near mouth of Cedar Creek in E 1/2 Section 18 (29-15W). Accessed by hiking along beach from La Push.

SUNSET CREEK PLACER. Located in Section 19 (29-15W).

RUBY BEACH PLACER. Located in E 1/2 NE 1/4 of Section 31 (26-13W) on tombolo between Abbey Island and Ruby Beach. The Ruby Beach Mining Company built a gold recovery plant in 1916 but never operated it.

SHI SHI
OZETTE
LITTLE WINK
YELLOW BANKS
STARBUCK / CEDAR CR.
SUNSET CREEK
JOHNSON POINT
RUBY BEACH
NORTH FORK
QUINAULT RIVER
MOCLIPS
COW POINT
OYHUT BEACH

Olympic Peninsula Ocean Beaches identified in Marshall T. Huntting 1955 Report as "Gold Bearing Beaches"

by Dan Youra   OlyGold.com

INFORMATION AND RESOURCES

REGULATIONS

Rules governing the activities of prospecting for gold and other minerals on Washington's Olympic Peninsula are regulated by a number of State and Federal Agencies.

GOLD AND WASHINGTON

The search for gold greatly affected the shape of Washington's history. Many miners bound for Alaska's gold fields in the late 1800s passed through Seattle and influenced the city's development. Interest in Washington's gold-bearing streams remains strong today. Improvements in mineral prospecting equipment make it easier for the casual or part-time prospector to engage in this activity.

DO I NEED A PERMIT TO PROSPECT IN WASHINGTON?

Since 1980, a permit (the Hydraulic Project Approval, or HPA) has been required from the Washington Department of Fish and Wildlife (WDFW) to mineral prospect or placer mine. Mineral prospecting and placer mining activities can harm fish and their habitat if not conducted properly. Limitations in an HPA are designed to protect fish and fish habitat while still allowing as much activity as possible. Most mineral prospecting and placer mining activities are permitted through the Gold and Fish pamphlet. You can print a copy of the pamphlet or request one from a WDFW office.

WASHINGTON STATE PERMITS AND REGULATIONS

In order to prospect for gold and other minerals in Washington State, a prospector must know and follow the rules governing mineral extraction. For answers about the laws the best source of information is "Gold and Fish: Rules and Regulations for Mineral Prospecting and Placer Mining" published by Washington Dept. of Fish and Wildlife.

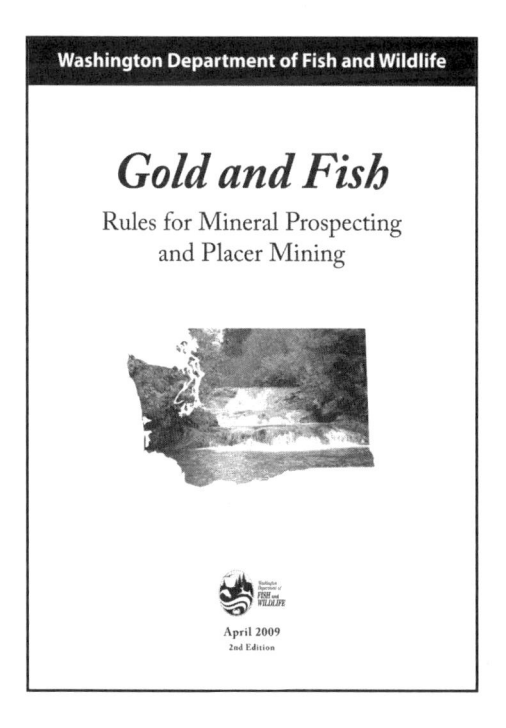

Washington Department of Fish and Wildlife

Gold and Fish
Rules for Mineral Prospecting and Placer Mining

April 2009
2nd Edition

Download "Gold and Fish: Rules and Regulations for Mineral Prospecting and Placer Mining" at: http://wdfw.wa.gov/habitat/goldfish/

The 2009 Gold and Fish pamphlet replaces all previous editions and will remain valid until the Washington Department of Fish and

Wildlife (WDFW) publishes a new edition. The rules contained in it were developed to protect fish and their habitats. This pamphlet serves as your Hydraulic Project Approval (HPA) for the types of mineral prospecting and mining activities described in it. You must follow the rules in the pamphlet when you conduct those projects in Washington.

This pamphlet includes the mineral prospecting rules under the Washington Administrative Code (WAC) available online at http://apps.leg.wa.gov/wac/ under WACs 220-110-020, -030, -031, -200, -201, -202, and -206. The rules were adopted by the Washington Fish and Wildlife Commission on November 8, 2008 and are effective April 3, 2009. The rules will remain in effect until modified or rescinded by the Commission. These rules do not relieve you from obtaining landowner permission and any other necessary permits before conducting any mineral prospecting activity. You must also follow the rules and regulations of tribal, local, federal, and other Washington state agencies. You may print out the Gold and Fish pamphlet from this website or request one from a WDFW office.

WHAT'S IN THE GOLD AND FISH PAMPHLET?

Mineral prospecting and placer mining is allowed under the Gold and Fish pamphlet with certain restrictions. There are two categories of prospecting:

1. You can use pans; spiral wheels; and smaller sluices, concentrators, mini rocker boxes, and mini high-bankers in certain portions of most locations year-round.

2. You can use pans; spiral wheels; larger sluices, concentrators, rocker boxes, and high-bankers; suction dredges; power sluice/suction dredge combinations; high-bankers; and power sluices only at specified locations and during certain times of the year.

Any number of individuals of any age may work at excavation sites.

No work on unstable slopes.

Ganged equipment may be used, up to a certain size.

Only larger prospecting equipment must be separated by 200 feet.

Work times are based on updated data.

Simplified screening criteria.

Maximum dredge nozzle size is five and a quarter inches.

Pressurized water may be used for leveling tailings and for crevicing.

If you want to conduct mineral prospecting or mining activities at different times or locations, or with different equipment than allowed in this pamphlet, you must apply for a separate, written HPA. You will receive an HPA if WDFW can determine that your proposed activity does not harm fish life.

You may request a written HPA by submitting a complete application to WDFW. The application form is titled "Joint Aquatic Resources Permit Application" (JARPA). The JARPA and instructions are available online at **www.epermitting.org.** You can also call the Office of Regulatory Assistance at **(800) 917-0043** or **(360) 407-7037**, or send an email to **help@ora.wa.gov**.

Several other state and federal agencies have an interest in mineral prospecting and placer mining, and may require a permit:

U.S. Army Corps of Engineers

U.S. Bureau of Land Management

U.S. Forest Service

National Marine Fisheries Service

U.S. Fish and Wildlife Service

National Park Service

Washington Department of Ecology

Washington Department of Natural Resources

Washington State Office of Archaeology and Historic Preservation

Washington State Parks and Recreation Commission

Local jurisdictions and tribal governments may also require permits. Contact these agencies directly (see the Gold and Fish pamphlet for contact information) or the Washington State Office of Regulatory Assistance at **(800) 917-0043**.

PENALTIES

Under Washington state law (RCW 77.15.300), it is a gross misdemeanor to conduct mineral prospecting activities when a Hydraulic Project Approval (HPA) is required without first having obtained one from the Washington Department of Fish and Wildlife (WDFW). It is also a gross misdemeanor to violate any requirements or conditions of the HPA. The maximum penalty for a gross misdemeanor is imprisonment for one year in jail and a $5,000 fine.

Under RCW 77.55.291, failure to comply with the provisions of the Gold and Fish paphlet or the rules it contains could result in a civil penalty of up to an additional $100 per day. WDFW will impose the civil penalty with an order in writing delivered by certified mail or personal service to the person who is penalized. The notice will describe the violation, identify the amount of the penalty and how to pay the penalty, and identify informal and formal appeal rights for the person penalized. If the violation is an ongoing violation, the penalty shall accrue for each additional day of violation. For ongoing violations, the civil penalty may continue to accrue during any appeal process unless the accrual is stayed in writing by WDFW.

The civil penalty order will be final and unappealable unless it is appealed in a timely manner as described in WAC 220-110-340 or 220-110-350. If appealed, the civil penalty becomes final upon issuance of a final order not subject to any further administrative appeal. When a civil penalty order becomes final, it is due and payable. If the civil penalty is not paid within thirty days after it becomes due and payable, WDFW may seek enforcement of the order under RCW 77.55.291 and 34.05.578.

DEFINITIONS OF TERMS

The following definitions apply to mineral prospecting activities that you conduct under authorization of the mineral prospecting rules and this pamphlet. Terms in this pamphlet that are in bold font are defined here.

Abandoning an excavation site — Not working an excavation site for 48 hours or longer.

Aggregate — A mixture of minerals separable by mechanical or physical means.

Artificial materials — Clean, inert materials that you use to construct diversion structures for mineral prospecting.

Bank —Any land surface above the ordinary high water line that adjoins a body of water and contains it except during floods. Bank also includes all land surfaces of islands above the ordinary high water line that adjoin a body of water and that are below the flood elevation of their surrounding body of water.

Bed —The land below the ordinary high water lines of state waters. This definition shall not include irrigation ditches, canals, storm water run-off devices, or other artificial watercourses except where they exist in a natural watercourse that has been altered by man.

Boulder —A stream substrate particle larger than ten inches in diameter.

Classify — To sort aggregate by hand or through a screen, grizzly, or similar device to remove the larger material and concentrate the remaining aggregate.

Concentrator — A device used to physically or mechanically separate the valuable mineral content from aggregate.

Crevicing — Removing aggregate from cracks and crevices using hand-held mineral prospecting tools or water pressure.

Dredging — Removal of bed material using other than hand-held tools.

Equipment — Any device powered by internal combustion; hydraulics; electricity, except less than one horse power; or livestock used as draft animals, except saddle horses; and the lines, cables, arms, or extensions associated with the device.

Excavation site — The pit, furrow, or hole from which you remove aggregate to process and recover minerals or into which wastewater is discharged to settle out sediments.

Fish life — All fish species, including but not limited to food fish, shellfish, game fish, and other nonclassified fish species and all stages of development of those species.

Fishway — Any facility or device that is designed to enable fish to effectively pass around or through an obstruction without undue stress or delay.

Food fish — Those species of the classes Osteichthyes, Agnatha, and Chondrichthyes that shall not be fished for except as authorized by rule of the director of WDFW.

Frequent scour zone — The area between the wetted perimeter and the toe of the slope, comprised of aggregate, boulders, or bedrock. Organic soils are not present in the frequent scour zone.

Game fish — Those species of the class Osteichthyes that shall not be fished for except as authorized by rule of the Washington Fish and Wildlife Commission.

Ganged equipment — Two or more pieces of mineral prospecting equipment coupled together to increase efficiency. An example is adding a second sluice to a highbanker.

Gold and Fish pamphlet ("pamphlet") — A document that details the rules for conducting small-scale and other prospecting and mining activities, and which serves as the hydraulic project approval for certain mineral prospecting and mining activities in Washington state.

Habitat improvement structures or stream channel improvements — Natural or human-made materials placed in or next to bodies of water to make existing conditions better for fish life. Rock flow deflectors, engineered logjams, and artificial riffles are examples.

Hand-held mineral prospecting tools — Tools that you hold by hand and are not powered by internal combustion, hydraulics, or pneumatics. Examples include metal detectors, shovels, picks, trowels, hammers, pry bars, handoperated winches, and battery-operated pumps specific to prospecting; and vac-pacs.

Hand-held tools — Tools that are held by hand and are not powered by internal combustion, hydraulics, pneumatics, or electricity. Some examples of hand-held tools are shovels, rakes, hammers, pry bars, and cable winches. This definition does not apply to hand-held tools used for mineral prospecting. See "hand-held mineral prospecting tools".

Hatchery — Any water impoundment or facility used for the captive spawning, hatching, or rearing of fish and shellfish.

High-banker — A stationary concentrator that you can operate outside the wetted perimeter of the body of water from which the water is removed, using water supplied by hand or by pumping. A high banker consists of a sluice box, hopper, and water supply. You supply aggregate to the high-banker by means other than suction dredging. This definition excludes rocker boxes.

High-banking — Using a highbanker to recover minerals.

Hydraulic project — Construction or performance of other work that will use, divert, obstruct, or change the natural flow or bed of any of the salt or fresh waters of the state.

Hydraulic Project Approval (HPA) —

(a) A written approval for a hydraulic project signed by the director of WDFW or the director's designates; or

(b) A printed Gold and Fish pamphlet issued by WDFW which identifies and authorizes specific minor hydraulic project activities for mineral prospecting and placer mining.

Job site — The space of ground including and immediately adjacent to the area where work is conducted under the authority of an HPA. For mineral prospecting and placer mining projects, the job site includes the excavation site.

Joint Aquatic Resources Permit Application (JARPA) — A form provided by WDFW and other agencies which an applicant submits when requesting a written HPA for a hydraulic project.

Lake — Any natural or impounded body of standing freshwater, except impoundments of the Columbia and Snake rivers.

Large woody material — Trees or tree parts larger than four inches in diameter and longer than six feet, and rootwads, wholly or partially waterward of the ordinary high water line.

Mean higher high water (MHHW) — The tidal elevation obtained by averaging each day's highest tide at a particular location over a period of 19 years. It is measured from the mean lower low water = 0.0 tidal elevation.

Mean lower low water (MLLW) — The 0.0 tidal elevation. It is determined by averaging each day's lowest tide at a particular location over a period of 19 years. It is the tidal datum for vertical tidal references in the saltwater area.

Mineral prospect(-ing) — To excavate, process, or classify aggregate using hand-held mineral prospecting tools and mineral prospecting equipment.

Mineral prospecting equipment — Any natural or

manufactured device, implement, or animal (other than the human body) that you use in any aspect of prospecting for or rEcovering minerals.

Mining — The production activity that follows mineral prospecting.

Ordinary high water line (OHWL) — The mark on the shores of all waters that will be found by examining the bed and banks and ascertaining where the presence and action of waters are so common and usual and so long continued in ordinary years, as to mark upon the soil or vegetation a character distinct from that of the abutting upland, provided that in any area where the ordinary high water line cannot be found, the ordinary high water line adjoining saltwater shall be the line of mean higher high water, and the ordinary high water line adjoining freshwater shall be the elevation of the mean annual flood.

Pan — An open metal or plastic dish that you operate by hand to separate gold or other minerals from aggregate by washing the aggregate.

Panning — Using a pan to wash aggregate.

Person — An individual or a public or private entity or organization. The term "person" includes local, state, and federal government agencies and all business organizations.

Placer — A glacial or alluvial deposit of gravel or sand containing eroded particles of minerals.

Power sluice — High-banker

Prospect(-ing) — The exploration for minerals and mineral deposits.

Redd — A nest made in gravel, consisting of a depression dug by a fish for egg deposition, and associated gravel mounds.

Riffle — The bottom of a concentrator containing a series of interstices or grooves to catch and retain a mineral such as gold.

River or stream — See Watercourse.

Rocker box — A nonmotorized concentrator consisting of a hopper attached to a cradle and a sluice box that you operate with a rocking motion.

Saltwater area — Those state waters and associated beds below the ordinary high water line and downstream of river mouths.

Shellfish — Those species of saltwater and freshwater invertebrates that shall not be taken except as authorized by rule of the director of WDFW. The term "shellfish" includes all stages of development and the bodily parts of shellfish species.

Slope — Any land surface above the frequent scour zone and wetted perimeter that adjoins a body of water. Slope also includes land surfaces of islands above the frequent scour zone that adjoin a body of water; or a stretch of ground forming a natural or artificial incline.

Sluice — A trough equipped with riffles across its bottom which you use to recover gold and other minerals with the use of flowing water.

Spiral wheel — A hand-operated or battery-powered rotating pan that you use to recover gold and minerals with the use of water.

Stable slope — A slope without visible evidence of slumping, sloughing, or other movement. Stable slopes will not show evidence of landslides, uprooted or tilted trees, exposed soils, water-saturated soils, and mud, or the recent erosion of soils and sediment. Woody vegetation is typically present on stable slopes.

Suction dredge — A machine that you use to move submerged aggregate via hydraulic suction. You process the aggregate through an attached sluice box for the recovery of gold and other minerals.

Suction dredging — Using a suction dredge for the recovery of gold and other minerals.

Tailings — The waste material that remains after you process aggregate for minerals.

Toe of the bank — The distinct break in slope between the stream bank or shoreline and the stream bottom or marine beach or bed, excluding areas of sloughing. For steep banks that extend into the water, the toe may be submerged below the ordinary high water line. For artificial structures, such as jetties or bulkheads, the toe refers to the base of the structure, where it meets the stream bed or marine beach or bed.

Toe of the slope — The base or bottom of a slope at the point where the ground surface abruptly changes to a significantly flatter grade.

Unstable slope — A slope with visible evidence of slumping, sloughing, or other movement. Evidence of unstable slopes includes landslides, uprooted or tilted trees, exposed soils, watersaturated soils, and mud, or the recent erosion of soils and sediment. Woody vegetation is typically not present on unstable slopes.

Vac-pac — A motorized, portable vacuum used for prospecting.

Watercourse and River or stream — Any portion of a channel, bed, bank, or bottom waterward of the ordinary high water line of waters of the state, including areas in which fish may spawn, reside, or pass, and tributary waters with defined bed or banks, which influence the quality of fish habitat downstream. This includes watercourses which flow on an intermittent basis or which fluctuate in level during the year, and applies to the entire bed of such watercourse whether or not the water is at peak level. This definition does not include irrigation ditches, canals, storm water run-off devices, or other entirely artificial watercourses, except where they exist in a natural watercourse that has been altered by humans.

Waters of the state or State waters — All salt waters and fresh waters waterward of ordinary high water lines and within the territorial boundaries of the state.

Wetted perimeter — The areas of a watercourse covered with flowing or nonflowing water.

Woody vegetation — Perennial trees and shrubs having stiff stems and bark. Woody vegetation does not include grasses, forbs, or annual plants.

ORGANIZATIONS

OLYMPIC PENINSULA TREASURE HUNTERS, 160 E Shady Valley Lane, Allyn, WA 98524. (360) 830-4709. Meets first Wednesday of each month at 7:30pm at Pinewood Manor Apt Rec Room, 280 Sylvan Way, Bremerton.

HOOD CANAL DETECTORISTS CLUB, 161 N.E. Mahonia, Belfair, WA; (360) 275-3856. Sunday of each month at 2pm at the Belfair Fire Hall, 460 Old Belfair Hwy, Belfair.

SEATTLE GOLD RUSH MUSEUM

SEATTLE KLONDIKE GOLD RUSH MUSEUM. Pioneer Square, 319 Second Ave. South, Seattle, WA. Visitor Information: (206) 220-4240. http://www.nps.gov/klse/

PENINSULA MUSEUMS

CLALLAM COUNTY MUSEUM. Port Angeles. Visit in Port Angeles, known as "The Center of Some Where"

JEFFERSON COUNTY HISTORICAL SOCIETY AND MUSEUM. Port Townsend. Visit in City Hall in Port Townsend.

GRAYS HARBOR MUSEUM, Grays Harbor

MASON COUNTY HISTORICAL MUSEUM, Shelton

BIBLIOGRAPHY

Gold Mining in Washington State - Yesterday and Today, Ken and Vida Martin, Golden Treasures Publishing, P.O. Box 1703, Stanwood, WA 98292. ISBN 0-9643300-0-8. LOC #94-78727 [ed. note: 122 page book sells on Amazon between $76.00 and $145.00]

Gold Mining in The 21st Century, Dave McCracken, [ed. note: book sells on Amazon for $35.95 new, $76.00 used. Book outlines EVERYTHING a beginner will need and want to know about getting started at gold mining today,]

Gold! Finding Gold in Washington State, Sean T. Taeschner, M.Ed., Order from Sean T. Taeschner, 30846 229 Pl. SE., Black Diamond, WA 98010. (360) 886-1262. [ed. note: book sells on Amazon for $12.55 new]

Exploring and Mining Gems and Gold in the West, Fred Rynerson. Author includes "the savage wilderness and rain forests of the Olympic Peninsula in Washington" [ed. note: paperback book sells on Amazon for $12.95 new]

Placer Gold Mining in Washington, Wayne S. Moen, [ed. note: this book is out of print with very limited availability]

You Can Find Gold: With a Metal Detector (Prospecting and Treasure Hunting) by Charles Garrett and Roy Legal (Paperback $9.95 - Nov 1995)

Gold! Gold! How and Where to Prospect for Gold (Prospecting and Treasure Hunting) by Joseph F. Petralia, Jill Applegate, and Susan Neri (Paperback $10.36 - Jan 1, 2006)

Mines and Minerals of Washington by George Bethune, Olympia: O.C. White, State Printer. 1891.

A Summary of Mining in the State of Washington. Bulletin No. 4. Seattle: Published by the University. Nov. 1918.

PENINSULA ATTRACTIONS

ART
Olympic Art Gallery
Quilcene **360-765-0200**
OlympicArtGallery.com

CASINO
The Point Casino Restaurant
Kingston, (360) 297-0070
The-Point-Casino.com

GROCERIES
Aldrich's Port Townsend
(360) 385-0500
Aldrichs.com

INN
Harborside Inn Port Townsend
(800) 942-5960
Harborside-Inn.com

MARITIME
Wooden Boat Foundation
Port Townsend, (360) 385-3628
WoodenBoat.org

MOTEL
Forks Motel in Forks
(800) 544-3416
ForksMotel.com

MUSIC
Olympic Music Festival
Center, Concerts on weekends
June-Sept. 360-732-4200
OlympicMusicFestival.org

REAL ESTATE
Coldwell Banker Settlers
Brinnon (360) 796-4900
CBSettlers.com

RESORT
Lake Crescent Lodge
On Lake Crescent in ONP.
Port Angeles. (360) 928-3211
LakeCrescentLodge.com

RESTAURANT
Public House Port Townsend
(360) 385-9708
ThePublicHouse.com

TOURS
All Points Charters & Tours
North Peninsula. 360-565-1139.
GoAllPoints.com

TRANSIT
Jefferson Transit
Port Townsend
Port Angeles. (360) 385-4777
JeffersonTransit.com

WHALE WATCHING
Puget Sound Express
Port Townsend, seasonal trips to
San Juan Islands. 360-385-5288.
PugetSoundExpress.com